Time Is Always Now

TIME
IS ALWAYS NOW

POEMS BY
Rebecca Starks

ABLE MUSE PRESS

Printed in the United States of America

Library of Congress Control Number: 2019937309

ISBN 978-1-77349-041-0 (paperback)
ISBN 978-1-77349-042-7 (digital)

Cover image: "Surtsey – Plants" by Thorunn Bara Bjornsdottir

Cover & book design by Alexander Pepple

Able Muse Press is an imprint of *Able Muse*: A Review of Poetry, Prose & Art—at www.ablemuse.com

Able Muse Press
467 Saratoga Avenue #602
San Jose, CA 95129

for my family

Acknowledgments

My grateful acknowledgments go to the editors of the following publications where these poems, some in earlier versions, first appeared:

Antiphon: "Postpartum"

Baltimore Review: "The More Things Change"

The Best of the Burlington Writers Workshop 2014: "Only Child" and "Decoy"

The Carolina Quarterly: "Out of Many, One"

Cider Press Review: "On Tidying Up"

Crab Orchard Review: "Examination of Mono Lake"

Grey Sparrow Journal: "Felt Most in Its Absence"

The Hopper: "Measure My Song"

Mezzo Cammin: "Eastward" and "When It Was Time"

Naugatuck River Review: "Assumption"

The Ocean State Review: "Hansel's Gretel"

The 2River View: "How a Mother Loves"

The Raintown Review: "The Long View"

Rattle: "Politicians" and "Open Carry"

Rust + Moth: "Ripe"

The Sow's Ear Poetry Review: "Thrown," "Diagonal," and "Book of the Dead"

Stonecoast Review: "Music Lesson" and "Arion as a Child"

SHARKPACK Poetry Review Annual: "Evening Alone in a City I Once Lived In"

Slice Literary: "Cemetery at White Point"

The Sunday Oregonian: "Thirty-Five"

Valparaiso Poetry Review: "If This Be the Season"

I'm deeply grateful to my parents for a childhood full of books, poems, art, music, and nature; to my siblings, for peopling this world; to my friends, near and far, and in particular Deirdre Lockwood, for helping me right and write my life; and I'm grateful as Bottom's Dream to Andy, from Coney Island to Cannon Beach to Snipe Ireland Road, for encouraging me to take my time; and to our children, for making each day new.

Especial thanks to others who helped keep alive and shape this book: mentor David Biespiel and the Attic Institute; early readers Wendy Willis, Dorothy Weicker, and Karin Gottshall; Paulann Petersen, Josh Booton, Gary Margolis, Julia Shipley, Partridge Boswell, Chard deNiord, and Baron Wormser, for their encouragement and guidance on individual poems; fellow members of the Burlington Writers Workshop for their careful feedback and camaraderie; the many editors and poets I learned from while working on *Mud Season Review*; my friends from Burlington Co-housing, my third and best university; artist Thorunn Bara Bjornsdottir for her gift of the cover image; and above all Maggie Smith, for helping me find the figure in the stone, and Alex Pepple at Able Muse, for his skill and grace in giving it life.

There are a few poets whose work I have long wished to see collected into a first book. Rebecca Starks is high on the list. Her intelligence and talent are beyond dispute. She has survived the swarms of contemporary American poetry of the last twenty years, that manic lurching from one aesthetic to another and the pressure of the new and the shocking, by remaining unhurried.

It's a quality of mind that reflects her strengths as a poet: figurative, emblematic, elegant, with poems that dramatize rapid movement from observed detail to mature insight.

Rebecca Starks writes with a sense that time can be stopped in a poem, lives suspended and drawn inward, even in the most aimless moments, where emotional potency is undeniable and marred feelings leave unforeseen imprints on the eyes and heart until you

> . . . walk away, crossing the tracks, arms free
> to cradle your own problems, your own needs—

There's a wonderful clarity to *Time Is Always Now*, an electricity that feels bright and wild. It's to be found in the roadsides and a robin's "clutch," in the retina that "registers pain," in the sky at dusk and the "months of mud." It's to be found in the examination of pollution and

> the skull-and-bone chapel
> mortared as Évora's *memento mori*
> under the epigraph Time Immemorial.

Her alertness demands purpose from her subjects which seem always in danger of being under threat, so that the

                            raw
sheering thrust of power
jangles me until I'm
any civilian cowering anywhere,
hands pressed to my ears
only making the pulse of terror
more interior.

This sort of concentration radiates in a poem like "Lament at Exxon":

You think of it at the gas station
pumping gas, keeping the pump
between you and a man doing the same,
now that you've both looked
and looked away in relief.

Maybe it's only the transition that's hard.
Lately you can't bear to see yourself
in the flesh, even a glimpse
like handling a quartered chicken
while the oven preheats.

So it was your own body you loved,
as seen and felt by lovers.
Just look at the middle-aged earth,
its warming at flashpoint.
You catch the man's eye again—

he's known it for thirty years.
If you don't believe your body
loves you back, what can you love?
You replace the nozzle, the cap.
What but your body can you give back?

What I admire in this kind of writing, as in so many other poems in this book, is the way she plays on contradictions between snapshots of private existence and public experience, between desires and disappointments—and in the nuanced and obviously concentrated way she turns a poem's inquiry from hand to eye to inner mind.

In these deeply moving poems, incongruities are undeniably real. You get the feeling of a life being written before your eyes, with all its occasional dignity and awkwardness. Over this lie landscapes of complex relations, a flickering between time and place. It is clear how much, intuitively or not, Emily Dickinson has meant to her—her probing of a moment, so that the never-quite-final construction of her attempts to affix it echoes Dickinson's own mistrust before her poems.

How can a poet be certain, and make sure you are certain, what is there? For Rebecca Starks, the problem is troubling, because she chooses subjects in motion—tree buds, fairy tales, animal tracks, brain damage, war, children, America's contradictions, violent impulses, art, poets, politicians, and things that can't be named—the opposite of Dickinson's still lives.

The title of this book says it best: time is always now. Time exists before our eyes. We are reminded, in this book, that poetry is both mirror and window. Through poems—with a poet with an extraordinary talent for metaphor like Rebecca Starks, that is—we accept the invitation to correlate and connect.

I greet these poems with so much enthusiasm—these poems which crave, clarify, and propose sublime ways to become refreshed in our most confused times.

David Biespiel
Portland, Oregon
2019

Contents

I

II

. . . we're forced to begin
In the midst of the hardest movement,
The one already sounding as we are born.

—Adrienne Rich

Time Is Always Now

I

The More Things Change

Every revolution ends, or it begins, in memory. . . .
            —Larry Levis

All the news in December is tree buds.
After a warm spell, the ground's sodden give
is a springboard for global speculation:

everything cellular deems it's spring—
as if for longer than living memory,
leaves haven't prepared against their brittle fall
the bulletin of their bursting forth again.

All the news in February is bird song,
as if it didn't break the ice each year,
the cardinal's *Do what you know, you don't know*—

as if no one up north had taken note
of how the *chits* resume when the light fans out
even as night's wings dip twenty below
and the lake stiffens under the air's touch.

I'd like to respond to the next-to-last caller:
look how, even taking the longest view
you want it immediate, chafe at delay.

You want to prove what we fail to imagine.
The revolution will begin with pruning,
anticipating memory—*We'll have to leave
that thought. We're out of time.*

The news, again, the eye-on-the-sky forecast,
variable clouds and sun, winds out of . . .
No, not out of time; helplessly in it.

Thrown

Those first days after time springs its catch
you're nagged by jet lag, a constant thirst

and asynchronous hunger, still restless
at lights out, then waking to your alarm

mid-dream, rocking, washed with a forgiveness
you hadn't known you were holding out for.

Still you come up short all day, the minutes
skipping in unremitting inspiration—

no time to breathe out artistry, only thaw.

—

But also the feeling you've been crowned, cut
loose from the dull rhythm, discharged by Osiris,

freed for the moment of your long too-much—
the sky climbing the nearest hill, pink and golden

first thing when you venture from your low cave,
the drip line as you duck off the front porch

melting pools in the strata of boot-packed ice,
the dog pouncing on each lost ball nosing up

like the first balloon breath of a crocus.

—

The walk to the car too easy, the air
balmy, shaming the outworn brace of defenses

still clinging to you: the chip on your shoulder
from months of subzero, the down coat you'll want

tomorrow, feeling the crunch underfoot.
But today the dirt road's turned to slip

on the mushrooming clay, each rut
shifting under the tires as you grip the wheel,

thumbs drilling down into the vessel being thrown. . . .

—

Not flung, but coaxed up wobbly as a fawn
finding its legs. Dimpled and then pinched to pour,

the way water everywhere streams from the rocks'
pitcher of clemency, as in your dream

passing through a doorway you met a friend,
and forgetting she was the one who turned away

from her betrayal, rushed to forgive her,
flooding with a too easy happiness,

carried away on the slant of its current
until wrenching the wheel back to center,

thumbs thrilling with the whir of stone—she was you.

Hansel's Gretel

Once they've gotten past the siren calls—wood thrush,
white-throated sparrow's whistle, the robins' alarm—
and waves of darkness slap against them, Hansel mistakes
a broken eggshell for a gleaming pebble.

Gretel suffers from heightened stereognosis,
seeing everything shaded by a hard pencil—
tree roots, acorns, her stone-bruised, impetuous feet—
her pupils vulnerable to the faintest light.

While Hansel stacks branches, Gretel gathers thin sticks
for kindling. She falls asleep to the fire's crackling.
The bread becomes gingerbread slab, the stepmother
a witch, her saccharine scolding burnt sugar.

The instant Gretel pushes her into the oven she wakes,
still hot with impulse. Hansel is blowing on embers.
Only when his story struggles does it come to him:
the thing to notice is that Gretel doesn't call her dream strange.

Only after having children does Gretel understand:
the thing to notice is that Hansel wants to go back.
As even now she wants to follow the dimples of light,
crouch under oak trees with the little round people

with hats, gather the dropped crabapples, dig for worms,
read out loud to her rabbits in their hutch at dusk
under the black cherry trees. Doesn't every home
hold them both: simmering love, simmering hate?

Even now she wants to run back to watch the pots.

The Long View

As far back as second grade, you remember
lagging behind your classmates with two boys,

one telling the other how his dad said to choose:
it's the ugly ducklings who grow up to be swans

like their mothers. "Then there's still hope for me,"
you put in, struck next by how they glanced at you

with surprise—that you'd spoken, or would say that
of yourself, or that they'd never considered you

a girl—but still your heart leapt they found you
already beautiful as Goldilocks

despite your bland forehead and pointy teeth,
not knowing yet how nearsighted you were

or what a long view they were taking, these boys
who would one day inherit their fathers' stocks.

Sunday Supplement

*The family usages, the language, the company, the furniture—
    the yearning and swelling heart,*

*Affection that will not be gainsay'd—the sense of what is real—
    the thought if, after all, it should prove unreal,*

The doubts of day-time and the doubts of night-time . . .

    . . . .

These became part of that child who went forth every day. . . .
    —Walt Whitman

        *I found the metal
on the street. It came from something
that had already failed.*
    —Thylias Moss

1.

Meaning to try a new church tomorrow
I get in bed early with *Small Congregations*,
the bookmark two days overdue,
my grip adding my whorls to the mass of Brooklyn
fingerprints fogging the contact paper
the covers are under as I am under them
    At two in the morning
the lines keep flocking to me, I roll them
on my tongue like swaths of sod gathering stones

13

the way shoes do, so you scoop them off
and carry the mules that should be carrying you
in that parable of fools

                             Among whom I number
my brother coming home from school, legs
swinging from the edge of the green vinyl seat
he slumped against, loafers dangling from his toes
like two ducklings paddling downstream
and then just one, the other sucked under
by a turtle, J.B., less bully than a tease—
before being winged hot-potato
wherever a hand flashed free, one eye
on the driver, one on baiting my brother
into flinging all he had at God
who ducked, gleeful, as the other shoe
flew out the open window
                               Nothing like
hanging up on the man you've got to talk to
as the payphone swallows your last change
of heart
        And J.B. knew it, turning
to slide the window shut before handing over
the loafer, lashes lowered in perfect contrition,
chanting *Hey, Will, this is a shoe—*
you've got one and I've got two!
while Stan kept looking straight ahead
at the rear view, foot grimly on the gas
not to laugh as the bus kept barreling,
wings tucked, two more miles

down Old Brownsboro, then let him off
hopping mad
                    Returning later with our mom
to trudge the roadside, kicking small
chunks of asphalt, skirting the matted scruff
of opossum—by the time they found the shoe
wedged in the bushes, so small and brown
and empty it could have held a robin's clutch,
he'd already outgrown it

2.

Things come back to you when you can't sleep
    No atmosphere, nothing burns up but you,
your ears funnels of loud croons, mocking
whoops and grunts of traffic backed and jacked
on Flatbush Avenue, drunks leaning
against the fat pillars of Checks Cashed,
the liquor store next door
                            It's four
in the Sunday morning and I haven't slept
more than an hour, even the heat waves
propagate sound so I turn the fan on high
washing white noise over everything
to short me out but it works like a bellows
    Because I've been reading
Thylias Moss I think categorically
white noise and hear the black music
below me and the Latin out back

and know it's the small segregations
you have to look out for, who you sit next to
on the subway, which neurons fire first,
how you line up books on your shelves—
my grandmother does it by color
but black and white aren't colors
                                    The pages
flutter against me contrary as a cat's tail,
I can't turn them slow enough
    Or lay to rest
the ghost of the Stoic who said all
emotion is nothing but a Fluttering
between you and your better judgment,
the plank's vibration just before you dive
into water shallow enough to kill you

Sound and Unsound cross a bridge,
if Sound falls off then what is left?

I could tread water all night
and I'm not a Stoic, or I wouldn't
need ear plugs to stop the sound
I can only compound, thinking
what else can I plug in
without bringing cops to the doorway again,
mistaking our hurry to reassure, stalling,
double-checking for violence curled up
domestic as a cat until the radio
static resolves: they have the address wrong—
Hurry!

3.

My roommate's electric toothbrush,
the blender, a never-used blow dryer,
the world band radio with poor reception,
the bunny-eared TV with none,
the Eroscillator—
                          That between you and me
my brother and I once borrowed a car
from Lucas—who took off on a long run
to the lighthouse, where we would pick him up
after browsing the aisles of Adult Books—
to buy and send to an angel cooped in the attic,
dreaming she still might fall to earth
    With windows papered over
it looked like they were renovating inside
but only from the outside, inside was all novelty,
eggs and mice and magic wands, and ours
the only car on Grand Street when it failed
to start up again, so we sat on the curb
eating Dunkin' Donuts from around the corner
thinking, Who could we call?
                              But Oscar
was on his way to five o'clock Mass
and wouldn't come near us, afraid we'd add
to his confessions, a long list already—
his list may be different from mine—
when a tin flew out a window
behind us, one story up,
*Dole*ing pale pear, orange peach
and red cherry confetti all around us

while the can hopped, rolled and rattled to a stop
we waited at
                    At last a door opened
and a man came out, retrieved the tin,
and crossed to the trashcan: bad aim,
imperfect contrition
                            The confetti stayed with us,
shrinking in the slant of late afternoon sun,
the street vibrating with heat making me think,
now I'd have to tell her how to use it
   The instructions say, *Use your imagination
and don't tell anyone*, but Lucas
must be ten miles out by now,
looking out for his car at the boarded-up
lighthouse

             The fan isn't oscillating
between anything, the sheets clingy with static
as I turn more pages like an engine turning
over

4.

     This is the year I live alone
without dissembling, letting my shame air out,
privately showing everyone the bruise
I had an affair and it ended
                    remorselessly
   Hair of the dog
we had briefly, his fur a curled blond

wool we carded and let float off
like drifts of cottonwood fluff gathering
in the roadside ditch where we found him,
after a week gone missing—shorn,
without his red collar—and brought him home
to bury in the backyard and cover with lime,
blaming ourselves and hating each other
even more when our mom went out
two days later to dig him up,
saying it hadn't looked like him, and now
I watch through the window of forgetting
whether we argued or let her argue herself

    Until the spade drops
bittersweet to earth like the bag of sugar
whipped from my dad's hands by a car
unseen as he stepped out into the street,
six years old and within an inch of his life

    When he got home, his mother had him
pick her out a willow switch
to teach him better judgment

                    It's too late,
I won't make it to a new church tomorrow,
I never have, but tomorrow I meant to try
the one on Sixth Avenue where they speak
Haitian creole
            Dreams are a creole, aren't they,
a mother tongue learned among strangers,
these late-night thoughts just pidgin
between me now and me then,

making tomorrow the next generation
drug of me
             I'll need to sleep in
one more Sunday

             Our dog's fur
teased soft as the pussy willow buds
that weren't out yet

5.

   But the reason I haven't slept is that
drifting off two hours ago
I woke up stifled, heart squeezed
between rage, self-doubt, and the indifference
of premature death, the room reeking of gas
   Chaos
           Brain damage
                   It's happened before
and no one ever smells the rot but me
   Like my mom once on codeine, my better half
rose, leaving its deadweight in bed
and made its way to the phonebook in the kitchen
and by streetlight found the number and dialed,
then waited an hour, windows open loud,
for two white men in white to buzz
   They'd left the gas detector in the truck
and the engine running, so all I could smell

was the exhaust they shook their heads with:
"It happens, people imagine things"
   Not me, I have no imagination,
only the memory of one
                        It keeps
playing in my head like a few bars of song
that won't resolve, how they condescend
back down the stairs and out the door
only to return grudgingly enthralled
to the divining rod, its blip of beeps slow,
searching and waning and then hot, hotter,
faster than a roadrunner the closer it gets
to Mama Duke's Soul Food
                        The loop
keeps playing with the fast heartbeat
of righteousness because I never got
to say *I told you so*,
just heard them between themselves:
"It's happened before, always Mama Duke's"

Knocking loud enough at last to conjure
an aproned man up from the basement, the porter
in *Macbeth* speaking Spanish, not speaking
at all, too groggy from the gas, the men
showing him he'd left a burner on all night:
"See? You'll blow the place up!"
as he nods and heads back down into the shadows
to sleep it off the next hour or two

I'd like to get some sleep too
but I'm too busy saving everyone's
life right now
              Hearing out
the Keyspan man who's worked there
thirteen years and always the night shift,
driving from way over there—as if
he doesn't get to start from where he is—
to way over there, border of Queens,
border of Coney Island, and everything
between
              "Always the top floor apartment,"
he'd said, when I said Top Floor,
the two of us staying on the first, martyred
by the sloping green stairs, his younger partner
out in the truck writing up the report—
I don't invite him up, he goes on talking

"You say, 'How long you been smellin' it?'
And they say 'Aw, three or four days'
and you say 'Hell'— they gotta call you
in the middle of the night. Or they wake up
and can't sleep so they start drillin' holes
and drill right through the gas main,
it's all leakin' out. Get in fights
and tear the stoves right out of the wall—
you wouldn't believe the shit you see.
There's guys go into derelict buildings
and steal the gas meters, leave the gas
just rushin' out. Boy you see everything."

Now he's seen me in my night shift,
I don't have a robe, there's no use
getting the paper, someone else would get to it
first; I just smell gas leaks,
the eggs we never found last Easter

Roll the stone back and let me sleep

6.

It's the one quiet hour of the night,
between four and five, the windows open,
a cross breeze trying to clear the air
as I listen for birds tumbling out their dreams
in bursts, in a hurry to remember
    Forgetting I'm not
in the suburbs of Mountain View anymore

Closer to five the morning traffic's begun
its shifts around the clock, even on a Sunday,
setting circadian rhythms to the clock of sound,
not light, sunrise an afterthought
    There's a stoplight
hanging on the wire right outside my window
and a 1/9 stop and a bus stop
and blockades of garbage lining my short block,
so the noise stops with me, starts to pass
but washes back a spell, idle engines

rocking like a porch swing about to launch
    I start to dream the train doors are closing,
hear the ding-ding "Stand clear"
and open my eyes wide to the noise real
and four floors down, sparking the dream
and waking me into a split universe,
the subway a super particle collider
trying to prove your existence, making it
as hard as possible
                       Just yesterday
before leaving the last stop in Brooklyn,
my thoughts were wandering from the weak nuclear force
to the Stoic warning never to say of a thing
I have lost it; say *I have returned it*—
when the black man beside me lunged
to grip the hard gums of the doors, yelling—
like my younger sister, three years old,
kicking at the door to see her grandmommy
when the live-in nurse locked her out,
until our dad came up the stairs two at a time,
mad enough as he once was to snap in two,
bare-handed the blades of kitchen knives
he'd warned Ela not to leave out:
they're still at the back of the knife drawer—
until both shuddering doors relaxed
to let a boy on the platform squeeze through,
ducking his head under his mother's arms,
the man and everyone shaking their heads
at Bad Parents:
                   "Let their kids get snatched

out from under them, don't pay attention,
leave them behind when the doors are closing"

The heartwarming, heartburning things
that lodge between you and your better judgment

7.

I look behind the curtain and there it is—
I don't have to check out the sun again,
it's been renewed
                    Not my sleep
                                  I keep
looking for some hole to burrow in
that isn't plugged with steel wool, drilling
my irritation into the brick wall
deep to where noise can still disturb,
where I can at least concentrate on it without
something fluttering from the fan, the corner of a poster,
either the Paul Klee or Last Judgment
Illuminated in an Initial A,
Angels blowing their horns to tell of news,
some of it good
                    Some of us are saved

I don't get to see how it happens
but Sunday's well along when I wake up,
the church crowd communing in earnest over
yellow grits and corned beef hash

burned on the bottom they'll never get to,
too busy swapping last week's news
to nod my way, glassy-eyed and hung-
over, stopping short of Psychic Palm
to count out change to buy the paper,
thin for a Sunday, missing its supplement

    I read the rest sitting
elevated on my one-step stoop,
trusting I'm the last one out the building,
leaning against the gray metal door
that will still be here in two years, five,
long after Mama Duke's Soul Food
has been erased by another bankrupt bank
of America, and I by a wife and mother,
but for now, that sop to better judgment,
I console myself, *It's happened before*,
and they, the faithful, *Always Mama Duke's*

Thirty-Five

So little makes it through a needle's eye,
Montale says of summer. Even less

knows when to double back, a skein of geese
drawn through the cottonwood clouds, all loft,

no seed. The camellias were badly sewn
on, the Italian plums, black walnuts,

magnolia leaves. . . . Now even the green pine's
needlessly dropping, its burnt matches

raked into haystacks that soak up the rain
spooling sidelong off gutters, squinting

to thread a thimble's pores. *You made it*—
but you haven't made anything yet

until a glint slinks up turning the earth's
rich selvage, yards from where you sank it,

and the double-knot holds, resisting the tug
not of what you hoped it would not.

Cemetery at White Point

So much of the earth that the earth does not feel their intrusion.
—*João Cabral de Melo Neto*

Passing over the crest we've gone back in time,
become unimaginable either way,
so far removed we can't feel our intrusion.

Tire tracks everywhere scar the unfinished land,
a craze of desire-paths overgrown with grass,
less corrections to the rectilinear

than errata: any would lead to the point
and yield a view of the blue-tinged North Mountains,
Tenerife and Sugar Loaf, silvered over.

I pick out what is white, but it's not enough
for a name: heads of gulls dotting the farthest
saddle of land; roots staving off erosion,

feeding clusters of chickweed flowers, daisies,
white clover with its spiderlike mandibles—
but also dandelions, harebells, blue flag;

round white granite stones studding the thin green sod
shorn where bedrock has collapsed into sea stacks—
the cairn looks unreachable, and we don't try;

clouds would be white, and waves breaking on themselves
in rough weather, fog gathering overnight,
snow in its season—this a clear summer day;

rich white of the seagull breasts wheeling, keening,
one bleating like a sheep after something lost,
leaving streaks of guano opaque to the light—

until we come to the solitary cross—
four feet tall, the solid planks nailed together,
at their crux a minuscule bronze crucifix—

standing guard over a cordoned stretch of grass
as if it lay fallow, or had just been sown—
a cemetery, then, whose low, hunchbacked stones,

no different from the others strewn about, must
mark graves of shipwrecked sailors, or hold their place.
Too little soil to cover a body here,

even beneath the sole engraved stone, the words
we stoop to glean—"Tomb of the Unknown Sailor"—
adding nothing, everything, to what surrounds,

like the brightest star in a constellation—
nearer than the rest, or immensely farther.
Someone must come, every few years, to repaint

what I knew at once to be the small white scratch
we'd spied from the top of Tenerife Mountain—
its name the Guanche words for *mountain* and *white*,

an island people who forgot how to sail
and sent young men off cliffs to speak with the dead—
through your binoculars shaken by the wind.

Book of the Dead

for A.M.

I scroll down through the newsfeed
the way my parents comb obituaries—
for the jolt of finding what I care about
or want to show I do—I do—by sending
flowers, clicking *like* once enough
nerve impulses fire; it has nothing to do
with liking. It's like giving out change
on the street, and over time I'm less
giving, distrusting the habit I'm feeding
in us both, how it inflates a currency
untethered from memory, until
I'm dismissive as one who's seen too much
of those who've seen too little
to align the telescope of need—
as with each touch on its siphon
the sea slug withdraws her gills,
until nothing can move her except bodily.
They'd have to pour their hearts out,
risky as that is—what if no one likes it?

Everyone agrees the book's a waste
of time, but you have to ask yourself,
if these are our lives, which is the waste?
I scan each page anyway, ever since a friend
died unnoticed, buried in my newsfeed

for a year and a half—first gone missing
for a week, then found in the Hudson,
his glasses on shore. I know how
he would have folded them, how his eyes
looked newborn without them.
They won't look at me anymore
except in profile, the one that's been left up
so I can tell his *ka* I'm thinking of him,
share my little news, my meals, answer
that post I neglected, wish him
a happy birthday the way we did
in our last exchange, throwing Dante
at each other, always reading too much
into words: *Nel mezzo del cammin,*
lasciate ogni speranza, a sua madre.
He doesn't like any of it.

But his is the page I fall open to
in this book of coming out into the light.

You Want to Travel Blind

Again I awakened
to light trying to thread my eye,
firefly in far Weehawken.

Light, I learned, is how
the retina registers pain.

I found this beautiful—
a detachment of angels
pinning a black curtain,

its heavy folds about to fall
too soon. Blind.

Three days I lay on my side,
then saw through a trembling halo
blue masks suspended

over the crystal eye
I couldn't close. I had to find

another lid to burrow
behind. A song. I woke to pain
but what is pain?

How blind nerves register
the tug of light?

All that month, Nina Simone,
and walking home re-bandaged
I stopped in the park

under elephantine branches.
I was old, falling apart.

I noticed the flap of shadows
before the leaves. It was spring.
I was twenty-two.

I put a hand to the immense trunk,
living totem to light. To light's angels.

Music Lesson

~~Wood throstle~~
Learning his whistle by ear
        from the ~~spool purl~~ spurl of the creek
Twisting the liquid filaments into
        ~~self-nullifying~~ self-harmonizing song

Practicing something he can't hear,
the tricky ~~bits~~ stretches,
the curl of ~~birch bark~~ a tendril
        around the divine

Like a girl holding still ~~long~~ longing enough
a morning glory encircles her finger

Not fiddling for ~~B-natural~~ the pitch
Letting it ~~fail~~ slide, taking it again
        from the twenty-fourth ~~measure~~ year
        with a new reach in mind
                        the canopy, the crown's
Tantalizing cadenza

~~Epithets Epiphytes of silence~~ Epiphytic notes
        hanging on air

The wind listens for ~~overtones~~ the ring
Not correcting fingering
Not turning the page

Green-eyed quiet
        in the flicker of leaves
Rosy-fingered hush above the leaf litter
        where ~~his mate~~ the mute nestles
Stunned mid-glissando
        by a ~~mirror of sky~~ glass mirage

Tempo ~~allegro~~ presto

Silence accompanying
~~The heart's The pendulum's~~ The heart's taut swing

On Tidying Up

after Marie Kondo

Let everything you own pass through your hands;
keep only what brings you joy.
You'll never have to do it again.

Live in a museum of your joy.
The stream-lifted pebble that still gleams, dry;
the shirt that fits just right in the bust;

the wallet that's served you twenty years;
the unexpected sight of your name,
that buried original self-delight. Joy.

But toss everything out blind
and you'll lug its ghost behind you forever,
the clutter of what you'll never know.

You who never wanted to live your life over,
moving always upwind,
picking up its scent only when the cut tin swings—

you wanted the possibility of being reminded
so you could forget it all.
Forget it, the way you forget your breath.

Let the true shades push forward
to drink from your favorite glass, thick-rimmed, blue,
all that has faded on the voyage home.

From childhood, whistling.
From school, the defenestration of Prague.
From your lovers, only your children.

You've named them all Joy.
From your living will, one sentence:
until nothing brings you joy.

II

Out of Many, One

Watchers of the sky at dusk—not fireworks, this time,
or a storm or meteor shower, not Shakespeare in the park
though there's a villain, and suspense, and a picnic—

we wait for the spectacle, already eight nights running,
of Vaux's swifts claiming an evening roost
during their mid-fall migration. By now the coming

cold has shrunk the metal lid of day,
sealing in the crickets and fireflies we'd caught
glints of before, the hillside hushed and settled

in a patchwork of blankets looking over Chapman
Elementary as the curtain of sky turns nebulous,
ushering into focus the massive brick chimney,

its tethered, magnetic mast poised to draw
stray iron filings from the edges of our view,
like flecks of broken burrs picked from wool

before gathering into fleece, teased thin,
washed and wrung, carded and spun, spindling—
nearing, then veering on its axis, narrowly

aware of the shadow hunched at the brick edge, still
skittish of the odds when each could be any—one—
plunging at last into the eye of its own storm,

the mass of ten thousand chittering swifts
draining with the light in a wide, coordinated gyre,
a runaway vertigo that suddenly sheers—

one pinked by the hawk's expert lunge, then gone.
Shadow lifted, the raised torch of smoke condenses
to descend in a funneling free-for-all fall

dwindling until the last one flutters feet-first
into the vertical burrow, huddled mortared
for the night in one body politic—

as we pack up the used plates and forks, pity and fear.

American Flag

No one believes it is happening.
I don't watch. Only the rain.

At 12:01 the dog licks my hand.
He senses my stillness

like a mutation in the air, in the meanings
of words and even in the logic

of storm windows wedged between us
and the warm winter day. By house

I mean republic. So quickly
assumptions change. Atoms

belong to you—but not you,
or you. How easy to prophesy!

With time all fears come true.
Still, the way you mourn after

is different from the way you
mourn before. The moment

blurs in the rain: the American flag.
All nations are mortal.

The dog wants to go outside.

Diagonal

Toes splayed, his face a mask of white-on-black,
the dog testing his weight keeps to my tracks
as I flatfoot up the trail, flinging up powder,
glittery and mostly fluff of breathy cold,
seven below when the wind's at my back.

I'm not the first—I notice *there are tracks*
and then the incurious ontology
of the phrase. If not God, something made them.
For once the hunter's logic stirs in me
as I look up at the cliffs and nothing looks back.

Rather than bushwhack I follow deer tracks—
comet trails leading up to sunken hearts
and at the bottom of their wells the cloven prow—
a long time, because this one went the way
I'm going, in a linear weave, pace slack

until he stepped to the edge of the footbridge
and changed his mind: turned and crossed the streambed
on his own. Diagonal from the path
appear muffled prints, a pair of coyotes
or a lone bobcat's out-and-back, tangled

as the early shadows of the dry-docked woods,
their doubled masts, spars, and rigging
reeled in by passing clouds. I tack upwind,
looking both ways, and cross carefully over
sociable mouse hops, two feet together,

pass a squirrel's scramble at the base of a tree,
then the bunched landings of a mustelid bound
from the yawn under one log to another.
Still only signs of life. It dawns on me
I got it wrong, that like the shadows pointing

to what blocks what blinds, glancing off
the cliffs' rim in a ricochet of second sunrise,
these tracks lead not to the body vulnerable
but to wherever—here—it's taken refuge.
Silence around me of my own making,

I hold it open to let the birds back in,
a wary one or two, then break for home—
mind leading the target, body dogged in its tracks.

Eastward

Two months of mud, and then we laid down sod
in swaths—a sudden spring of *Look, don't touch.*
All April, while roots soaked through the mulch,
Off! we trained the dog—off our four-month-old,
off squirrels, off cats—and then we mowed,
ramming the blades against the fatted flock,
and let our dog out back to romp in the shock
of blank lawn so long kept out of the fold.
Watching her crouch, dash, tearing up the grass,
teasing out its spring—I felt her release
catch in my throat and, shifting abruptly
my son forgotten on my hip, heard his laugh
like the first choked turn of the mower's scythe
as if a hand had lifted a rib from my side.

Assumption

As I slant up the wooded trail
this last day of August, my heels

for once undogged, eyes caught
by the spatter of each yellow

locust leaf—first disintegration
of summer—*I feel physically*

the top of my head taken off—
and cry out in a buried voice.

When I see what's raked my scalp
swoop up to a bare branch

and perch soft as a cat, head swiveled
to assess where it went wrong,

I hear my cry for what it was,
my skin pricked with instinct—

I'd known what mimetic warning
to send up to my scattered troop,

what howl: *Barred owl. Who looks,*
who looks, who looks for you.

His hunch—*this isn't*—leaves me
alive to the grip of why,

before the dying finish knowing
how, leaping the emphatic gap

they look back with Death's eyes,
terror at its clutch contorting to pity

for what they can't lift up.

Examination of Mono Lake

When the war is over, there will be time enough to pull
through the thread.
　　　　　　　—*the Sewing Machine Historian of Vilna*

1.

If lakes rise to patch where the land's rubbed thin
as the Paiutes tell it, then when your level falls,
has the land begun to heal, like skin?

Brine-fly eaters, you must mean—worth the salt
they seasoned with. By "worn" they meant no judgment,
no wound, but commonweal—how with each haul

the land changes hands that work its easement
beyond the shifting shore of its promised scope
until it shrugs them off, indifferent.

Mending has meant ripping old seams open,
wrecking the makeshift into haunts of trauma:
the shy migration of Wilson's Phalarope

denied vistas of the Sierra Nevada,
springs that cemented clouds of limestone
diverted to steam LA fitness saunas,

the pattern foraging beaks dart and sew
among the brine shrimp dilated and diluted—
California gulls, more poor historians.

2.

Given that a new ruling against pollution
windblown your way may reverse the trend,
how long a view should we take of this uprooting?

As long as you have a new frontier, you'll defend
to the death of what you meant to improve
the slide from shortsighted to cosmic end.

Late-combers of these shores who come to root
and thread their way among the ruined tufa staves,
blind to their futile prairie dog salute,

with each step send up swarms of flies in waves
that set, magnetic, in newsprint, raising a screen
between them and the lives it keeps at bay.

Pore too close, the letters start to bleed.
Tufa, light as loofa and opera buffa,
scrubs history clean. It isn't travertine—

curried and pounded to a smooth bouquet
by the palms and feet of a blind crush of pilgrims—
or sand that's pedaled into drifts, but beauty-

cum-junk. Beside the protean Colosseum—
gone from circus, fortress, monastery, to shrine,
quarry, cemetery; misuse to museum;

shroud to drop-scene clouds slip to change behind—
the lake is nothing more than rusted colander
sunk to reliquary of what it brines.

3.

Remember what Rodin christened his calling: *L'art
du trou et de la bosse*. The lump and the hole.
Do you consider yourself a sculptor?

*Only the vessel, if a lake can be vessel
of what it spurns, and drop without breaking.
The towers, though, could be my Gates of Hell.*

Castles of sand crumbling up, rude and vacant;
pitted, ragged crusts of sun-bleached plaster
poured over the muffled profile of the mason,

its congested, oncogenic vapor
lacking the bluster of skin or muscle, bone.
It has the look of pathos without nerves.

A witness to its menagerie—iguanas
and saints, koalas and hurrahs, jeers and ghouls—
glosses all but the sirenic yawns

that give him pause, like the skull-and-bone chapel
mortared as Évora's *memento mori*
under the epigraph Time Immemorial.

4.

The more you pause, the further on your journey
you'll be, the priest's grim poem ends—*i.e.*, near
Death. Who is this witness of whom you speak?

He's in a long hall of a thousand years.
Dragged to the light, his eyes track interstitial
holes in the round, each O despairing as it appears. . . .

None are copies, none originals;
curios, scraps of Darwin's *il-fa-presto*
pressed punctuated into quasi-fossils

whose Braille ripples with the account of a ghetto
sewn by a man with open-eyed needle—
make it quick. But all the wrongs he embedded

never threaded their way out of the cradle
he harrowed into light, forgetting that paper,
like all that's lived, is degradable.

Though within each shifting cell the inverse
is true: had he rigged its twisting ladders' rungs,
the exiled code might have been preserved.

5.

That binary record of life's extinction
assumes a mind to read it in the future.
If we don't colonize space, will there be one?

Single-cell fossils found entombed in the tufa
give clues to where to look for life on Mars:
in basins like mine where minerals intrude

and concentrate, until the hope they harbor
of a less common fate evaporates—
the same sun and meteorites bombard

us both. What's certain in this twilight age?
Coyotes running along the land's new scars
gorge on eared grebes where they once safely staged;

green rabbit brush takes cover, tipping its fur
in salt. Beneath the lake, bubbles of impatience
form testaments to what endures, while mirrored

on the surface hands lined like nets, or nests,
skim larvae quick as spirits, before they rise.
Gathering clouds unsecured as if to test,

a long red thread pulls through another sunrise.

III

Measure My Song

Out in the garden we're tying twine
for the tomato vines to climb up
out of sawn-off milk jugs,
little makeshift greenhouses
for the cold spring.

It's one of those clear mornings
the Lockheed Falcons seem to flock to,
as if preparing for desert skies,
or—on a joyride—for F-35s
two years down the road
and four times louder and harder to fly.
Surely they won't fly.

From beneath the power lines
we crane to see them,
small as deer flies, following the sound
they shed like a chrysalis—
there they are, two of them,
peeling off from each other,
splitting the sky.

—

After a minute the worst has passed,
like a contraction,
and bracing for the next
I think of Leo Lionni's worm
inching away from the nightingale
to measure the threat of its song.

I wonder how birds cope,
if they ever crash-land like whales
deafened by sonic booms
the Navy uses to train its ears
to pick up the subtlest
whispers from the quietest submarines—
or if it's so outside the birds' experience
their senses can't take it in.

For me, it's the opposite: that raw
sheering thrust of power
jangles me until I'm
any civilian cowering anywhere,
hands pressed to my ears
only making the pulse of terror
more interior.

—

When I take my hands away
there's nothing subtle or new
in the stillness—a few bird trills,
my breath, roots underfoot—
but an inner prompt.

Dear Lieutenant Colonel—
(the double title
raising the specter of Heller's
catch: if you protest
you protest too much,
but still I place my stone
on the grave of objection)
even the F-16s are too loud.

Dear Liberal Poet, he writes back
graciously that evening,
I will pass your note on—
right now I'm in the airport
welcoming home a young man
from his tour in Afghanistan.

After the boom subsides
I hear it, the distancing
rustle of the inchworm.

Politicians

They rely on your forgetting. They forget
themselves, or everything but. Around forever,
always the same, always distancing themselves
from who they were. Like the first secretary
of the regional party committee, in charge
of not adding iodine to the water
after Chernobyl, they aren't criminals
but products of their time. The time is always now,
the river from Pripyat through Flint conveying
the same products, made of cheaper ingredients
in deceptively slightly smaller packages
with new health claims. They want you to buy them.

They don't remember how the refrigerator died
one summer and they didn't get a new one
for a biblical seven years—maybe a few weeks,
they say now, unwilling to look at the proof,
the email where we refused to come home
until they bought a new one. My guess is it's
the suggestion of influence they mean to block out,
not the seven years they bought bags of ice
daily to keep a carton of milk from souring
in the freezer, and every so often a few pints
of Graeter's they ate all at once as it softened.
But the seven years had to go, too. It's a process. . . .

They couldn't decide what kind to get.
Most of the new ones were bigger and didn't fit.
Double doors, freezer on bottom, ice dispenser,
novelties they shelved as too radical a change.
We don't like the new one when we visit,
we can't reach things, rummaging, we bump our heads,
it takes up too much room but doesn't hold enough.
We haven't forgotten what the old one was like
or what sat where on the shelves: the Velveeta box
and pimento olives, Aunt Jemima's syrup
and Smucker's jam and gallon jugs of skim milk,
and margarine and D cheese, we called it, for its shape.
The Peter Pan in the cupboard never got old.

We're spoiled—now they stock our leafy greens
and grass-fed butter, the bread drawer rolls out
Great Harvest loaves instead of Roman Meal,
and in the cupboard low-sodium Progresso
pushes out Campbell's. That's progress. It feels like progress
until you look for a functioning can opener.
But I understand, with all due respect, why people
vote for their parents anyway. Because
you know them, they aren't so bad anymore,
they let you forget yourself. They were never that bad.
Though didn't they—did they really?—rent a car
every day for fifteen years, when theirs died?

They laugh.

Poem of Our Climate

Since the imperfect is so hot in us
          —Wallace Stevens

I learned it from the repurposed priest
who taught us European History,
as he looked up from a dreaded Purple Cow
(mimeographed sheet covered in his scrawl)
to digress: the three things not to be discussed
in polite company. My thoughts went Wild West,
saloon cowboys chastened by the gentle sex,
but now I hear the homophone, *disgust*.
Nothing ruder than a point of view—
before returning to Henry the VIII
sloughing off his wives in a series of bruits:
FAKE MARRIAGE! LOSER POPE! PATHETIC MORE!

That left the weather, but now not even that.
My father calls to report this March fourteenth
is the coldest on record. He remembers
forty years ago, the Ohio froze
and headlines warned of the impending ice age.
He read us by lamplight *The Skin of Our Teeth*.
He's learned from history we're always wrong,
or they are. He'll vote crude oil or no one.

Lament at Exxon

You think of it at the gas station
pumping gas, keeping the pump
between you and a man doing the same,
now that you've both looked
and looked away in relief.

Maybe it's only the transition that's hard.
Lately you can't bear to see yourself
in the flesh, even a glimpse
like handling a quartered chicken
while the oven preheats.

So it was your own body you loved,
as seen and felt by lovers.
Just look at the middle-aged earth,
its warming at flashpoint.
You catch the man's eye again—

he's known it for thirty years.
If you don't believe your body
loves you back, what can you love?
You replace the nozzle, the cap.
What but your body can you give back?

Open Carry

Las Vegas, October 1, 2017

What if each of their Lives had Stood,
a folded Umbrella, until that Day—

What if the National Umbrella Association
lobbied to repeal luck's laws
and we could open umbrellas in the house,
lay them on beds and give them as gifts—
and even on sunny days, carry them open
in night clubs and places of worship,
movie theaters and elementary schools,
offices and outdoor concerts—a real cause,
so we no longer had to leave them shut up
in closets or hanging on walls
or leaning against porch railings
or stashed in bedside drawers in hotels—
so that everyone could be prepared,
everyone saved, the black honeycomb
stand its ground shoulder to shoulder
against the cloud's dark motive—

It rains four inches a year in Las Vegas.
What if this isn't the time to talk about umbrellas?

I have one in my bag right now,
a Robinson, a Gamp, a spring-loaded automatic,
at a touch it will bloom
to receive the syncopated sound of rain
dancing, hopping on the taut roof
the way a gun can sound like firecrackers from the sky.
It's true there are still puddles and spray,
there is the lower half of you, the arm aches,
the skin blows inside out like a skirt in the wind.
Here and there a man tries to shield a woman,
covering suede and silk and hair
with his outspread body—

What if umbrellas don't keep you dry,
people do, and are broken trying?

Post-Patriotic Ode on Town Meeting Day

First time? Welcome to the democratic process.
I hesitate to fig-leaf my hand to my heart,
       Botticelli gesture I now confuse with kneeling,
head bowed, to propose: Will you, land of the free,
take me as yours? Surrounded by uniforms—
police, Boy Scouts preparing to be officers—
       I do what others do. It's been so long
I fumble after "under God," about to murmur
Thy kingdom come, Thy will be done. . . .

There's the car mechanic's wife, the librarian,
the neighbor behind the tripod, the math teacher
       without her dog, the couple whose house abuts the bridge.
For all. The veteran fire fighter stands up:
due to age, incapacity, they're short hands
to put on the Fourth. He can't speak to the future.
       He doesn't know what will happen—they've asked
and asked. They need someone to make the fries and donuts.
He shakes his head. If you can, sign up. . . .

A mother sitting by me on the hard bleachers
leans in to whisper, *Isn't it boring? The same*
hundred people every year. The same hundred people
       in every town—the retiree, the parent,
the business head, the suspicious. *Could you give*
an example of what's in the Two Percent
       Miscellaneous pie slice? Privately
I question the eighteen grand the police spent on gas.
Couldn't they go electric? Stop idling?

But they've been busy—spying stolen garden tools
in back of a pick-up, reviving a drugged male,
          processing unruly females, writing up mischief,
the petty, the dull, the brutal, the wrenching,
chasing down a mom abandoning her kids,
giving her a number to call. Last year, I read,
          the volunteer constable was called once
about a stray dog, gone when he got there. He looked for
more to do. This year, some barking dogs.

The budget discussion wraps up, and I realize
I've been using last year's summary as anchor
          when suddenly it predicts what will happen next, who
will propose we adopt a resolution
welcoming everybody to our town (pop.
one stoplight, one café). How 2017.
          This year we'd like to raze the Jonesville gun shop.
You could knock it down with a sledgehammer, the mother
assures me, getting up to leave.

I follow, and those who smiled in welcome turn now
to frown. A town meeting isn't a reservoir
          to take a dip in, the town a sleeper to kiss,
then hop on the highway. Hovering at the exit
I scan the list of births, marriages, deaths—
no one I know. On the curb outside I learn
          I voted for the wrong people and approved
the wrong funds, but the right ones carry the day, a rare
bright one, before the next nor'easter.

Escaping into acres of conserved woodland,
grateful but critical I find myself quarreling
        with the budget for snow, the wind's leadership, the low
priority placed on upkeep of the pines—
and looking at the sky through thinning branches,
slip on the balance sheet of old ice. Nudged by
        the dog I get to my feet slowly, resolving
like the constable to look for more to do, before
tomorrow's snow covers my tracks.

Democracy! Like two tear-streaked toddlers, willful
and fearful, you long to drop at the station once
        and for all and walk away, crossing the tracks, arms free
to cradle your own problems, your own needs—
but already the heart constricted, mind nagged
by all the police might not remember about
        rhythms of care beyond emergency—
garbled words tickling the ear, the bossy trust, the joy
of smearing painted fingerprints—

rush of relief like warm bathwater on your wrist
when the door swings open and you're run after, held,
        charged to take them back. Hefting one on your hip,
leading the other by the hand you let think leads you—
maybe you'd better after all.

Evening Alone in a City I Once Lived In

St. Michael's Promenade, Washington Heights

I don't have to look to know they're lovers
settling at the far end of my bench, inverse
shim unsteadying the view—the fortress of stones,

the ragged pyre, the gloomy river unprepared
for sacrifice—and then a breeze shaking down the brush—
the ram sent by Michael. Their silence tautening

wing screws of a flower press over the sun's petals,
the last of their pink absorbed by the small cloud
cupped like a hand smoothing the tousle of trees,

then lifting to turn the page.

IV

Only Child

The first spring Andy cleared the vines
that gave the tree its only green—
some twelve feet high and never pruned—
it sprouted simple, unlobed leaves.
We watched their light green glow unfold
in delicate tongues with curled tips
along a few weak, rain-soaked boughs
bent like whips of forsythia.

The second they began to bunch
and crowd enough we had no qualms
twisting sprigs from the longest branch
to test our local nurseries
and arborists we hoped could tell
its Latin or its common name,
but dovelike we returned each time
embellished by new ignorance.

Still Andy's suspicion—fruit tree,
bearing no fruit—until that fall
unshaded by its canopy
a large green pear, rock-hard, appeared
bare on the ground with broken stem
while in the tree, no sign of pears
but one torn white strip on a limb
where this one might have hung unseen.

Had some young boy like Augustine
returned it with remorse—lobbed it
over the wrong fence, giving us
this mistaken April hope of more?
Or had the tree spent all on this—
revived devotion pushing forth
more than a season's growth supports?
It kept, unripened, for a year.

Postpartum

Sitting up in bed nursing my son at night
the nothingness of it would sweep me away
following the distant whistle of the train—
clearer on winter nights, unmuffled by leaves—
passing through town as the milk passed through me,
impersonal as my son's averted eyes,
his hand pulling my hair taut to hold me there,
trickle and swallow, nursing my own black thoughts,
our oneness nothing but the ritual
blurring of broken time—I, the candle lit—
the bleakness of waiting to burn down to sleep
setting me by the door open to the dark
waiting for the dog to come in from out back,
listening for her jingle through the flicker of rain.

Parable of Two Sons

Because no altar of the nightly news
orients our unlocked cabin,
just four-point windows turning over
the local rocks—the pileated

woodpecker picking at stale sumac berries,
a wild turkey family
advancing their necks up over the hill,
a sharp-shinned hawk clutching a snake—

to prepare my sons for the wider world
at night I read them Bible stories
broadcast with modern facts and photographs—
a ram's horn, threshing tools, fig cakes,

the myrrh and makeup Esther likely used—
mulberry, henna, kohl—to win
favor for their people, and at the well
me with a nose ring like a cow's.

Story after story my firstborn shrugs off,
knowing seas part in a tsunami,
resurrection rouses from a deep sleep,
a sandbar affords a path on water,

until he loses his footing, the waves
close in and he falls silent

at Stephen's stoning, John the Baptist's head,
Jephthah's daughter's sacrifice.

Meanwhile his younger brother—favored, both
have taken note—who for some months
has asked for only one story, how we
became people from wild apes,

not fossil records and tectonic plates
but the turning, imaginal
discs in their slip—stops asking why and sinks
into the mystery of *story*.

When in the story, three times, a child dies,
each time he is restored to life
by Samuel, by Elisha, by Jesus,
I hear a release of breath, my son's

breath that would clear the heavens.

But Here There Are No Cows

You have to be ruthless, my friend
shakes his head when I confess to lazy
benevolence, not yanking up the tomato plant
sprouting where I let last year's tomatoes rot

where they fell—now encroaching on a row
of beets. Of course weeds will run rampant,
the produce suffer. But why do I have to be ruthless?

I never thin the carrots or the beets,
too pained by waste. It's why I poached a heart:
fear of squandering such capacity
for love. The popcorn kernels we tossed

in the compost have burst the wire cage
with pressing green. My father warned us
how the world can turn. You have to be cruel

to be kind, he'd chide his wife's reluctance
to instruct the milkman not to come inside,
the way he would do, Sam Loyding room on a shelf
in the fridge, but leave the jug in the metal box

out on the porch. She never did. We got our milk
from the store. *Are there any humans
who are like weeds?* my son asks—

one of his terrible questions like,
What does the inside of a bomb look like?—
and I falter. Should I talk of genocide, of empires,
or rehabilitate the weed—here first flowers,

with untapped healing properties? Because he sees
how we decide: to keep or discard, water
or uproot, nurture or slaughter, always

the fine distinction: good/bad, native/invasive,
paradise/parasite. We read in *Julie of the Wolves*
of the Arctic's widening circle of love,
and when we get gerbils, we stop killing mice

until we're overrun. A certain type of person
takes pleasure in insoluble moral dilemmas
ending like the boat scene in *Apocalypse Now*:

liberal meddling gets everyone killed.
They find it immensely satisfying
War is Hell. Others tear up garlic mustard
and plant bleeding heart along every border.

When It Was Time

We let her stalk through the garden's unmown grass
one last time, not that she could take it with her
but to set things right a quiet moment,
her drab gray softened to pastel calico
dappled in the evening's delaying light.
It wasn't hope we had kept alive
but the existential dread of ending,
not knowing when and having to decide.
Done with two shots: one to lull her into sleep,
the second to slow her breathing to a stop,
a sleight-of-hand designed to ease the guilt
of killing into some more natural
release, but all it did was hammer home
how much closer sleep is to life than death.

—

I felt how her soul had leavened her body,
half its usual size but heavier
than she had been for a long time, heavy
as when she slept or rested on me, content,
purring along to the hum of my concentration,
as I held her on my lap for the drive home
wrapped in a light blue towel damp with pee,
still warm; her face a stuffed animal's
I quickly covered up again, the whiskers
bent, eyes glassy, fur mashed, she'd been so real,
so loved, and in withdrawal from compassion

I was filled with a strange empty elation
striking a chord of comfort, terror, grief
that death was nothing I could ever hold.

—

Nothing makes us more primitive than a body
stripped of overlay of culture, soul,
in limbo between what we love and refuse
to be disposed of before we're ready,
before life swarms to fill the vacancy,
soil the misshapen hole we dug hastily
at dusk—the air the color of mosquitoes—
and fitted her in, still wrapped in the towel,
dirt pattering on her so carefully
groomed paws and ears, stretched legs, her spiny tail,
her salmon-striped rib cage we pressed a stone on
like kids to make a fossil overnight;
thunder drove us in, all night it rained, our son
rocked in the wake of a dream she was washed away.

Scarce from Its Mold

Always too long between visits home,
meanwhile making others do. Here our friends'
homestead churns out mutton and wool,

fertilized eggs and liver pâté:
a vertical monopoly on life
I've come to show my sons, too *greenhorn*

to know the word's meaning—tugging on me
like all that stands between them and flying
as we hover around the bee balm.

At the sight of something new we hush,
as if needed, gods dreaming a new species,
chimera of hummingbird, bee, moth—

"Behemoth?" Chris jokes in her wry way.
That unanswerable, but far too small.
It has to be a moth—but the wings hum

so fast their brick-red borders disappear,
the stripes warn *sting*—with that furred spindle
of a body, those feathered feelers.

It's still summer, soon slaughtering time
before the lambs teetering on their mother's backs
can cut their first incisors.

"Why can't you just say goodbye?" one son asks,
delight in clamber and gambol fading.
"Why do you have to keep talking?" Because—

you'll see, you'll do it too, afraid
you've seen everything but what you're afraid of
in every ending. I have him look closer—

the bees padding their holsters, the clearwing moth
inserting itself in a flower
it won't disturb, with just a forefoot, briefly

steadying itself with the taste of what it lives on.

Felt Most in Its Absence

In the Bible you read of the father's blessing
as something given once, to one son, binding—
Isaac's excuse to Esau—the heart not in
the second blessing, false as the mother's is
disguised. What I bestow is sleep: every hour
my son wakes I nurse him, cradle him, press
my hand on his back, leaving him what he wants
of me, and then I lie beside my husband until
his breath falls effortless, he'll think he's hugging me
all this time, though sometimes he's troubled
by dreams in which I'm unfaithful, and I know
why, as I slip out from under the yoke of his limbs
and go into an empty room to write, stilling
what's restless in me, willing the words to hold.

Ripe

How hard it is to take September
straight—not as a harbinger
of something harder.
          —Mary Jo Salter

The harvest must bring on these thoughts
of perfection: gold sungold, plump pumpkin,
thump of melon, tang of apples

ripening the air, milkweed letting down
its seeds, our sons relaxed and easy
in mind and body as infants' mouths

slipping from the breast, fists in bloom—
Around, the younger reads out loud,
moving his mouth like the word, seizing

with laughter—as the older plays Brahms,
leaning the violin flat for the high notes,
saying the crescendo's like in a book,

when you're afraid something bad
will happen—and I feel it—that vertiginous lust
of fear you'd almost rather get to the end of

than live with, that we all live with—
most as I pick up a light shirt, still warm,
from its tangle on the floor,

breathing the life that was just here.

If This Be the Season

Her mind moves now
from autumn leaves to milk.
The earth turns, too,
more quickly. Her grown
children come home again.
She slides in all four leaves.
Longest table, shortest day,
fattest tree to trim
and mist each night.
The milk's left out all week.
When they've gone,
she'll pour the curds
in a vase, setting to soak
the stems of dish-washed
silver until they bloom.

How a Mother Loves

When the dog disappeared out back, last May, fifteen years after they'd brought him home, she looked until she found him, down the hill and under some hemlocks where he'd lain down to die, the way animals do—she says she knew that's what he was doing—and though he was too big for her to lift and she had no cartilage in the joint of one hip she got him up the hill too steep to mow and into the house to his spot by the door and he lived there another week and a half, with her lifting him up with a towel each morning and hugging him to sleep at night, since he could neither stand nor lie down, nor remember what to let go of, to fall asleep.

Arion as a Child

When the house still hugs the day's heat
and my son wrestles sleep, I bring him down
       to watch the fireflies,

Turn off all the lights inside, out,
and sidesaddle him off the porch
       naked into the stars—

Some low, some high as the facing hills—
never where you last spotted them,
       flickering like heat lightning.

Wading barefoot into the dew,
my fingers brushing the fine Braille
       budding up from his skin—

A flash passes so close it streaks
like a meteor, and with a
       dolphin kick and quick breath

In he dives—and I dive after,
catching him up. We have these leaps
       in us, we hold these reins.

Decoy

Up on the barrens of Cape Breton
there's so much we can't name.

Mosquitoes tightly orbit our Tilley hats
as we hop on half-submerged stones and slip

on waterlogged logs bobbing under algae.
What were we saving our dry selves for?

A little newt, plastic orange, with a wobbly axis
waddles away under the shrubby growth.

A red lantern of double origami paper
hangs off a short stiff frown of stem.

I pry open one side of its mouth
and a fly purr-purrs out. You bend to look

and the flower snaps off like thin glass
breaking the distortion of its transparency.

We look around and it's the only one,
not something you want to hold or let fall.

You hand it to me and we trudge on,
boots squelching, torment in our ears.

At the base of the stem, we'd seen curled tongues
sprouting small sticky hairs: a pitcher plant.

Dozens of these dull-red lanterns. Then what
was the flower for? And the fly—if not

pollinating, then prey; instead of digested, saved.

"Sunday Supplement" on page 13: The phrase "indifference of premature death" alludes to a line in Chekhov's "A Boring Story," though I knew it from a church letter board's version: "Indifference of spirit is premature death."

"Thirty-Five" on page 27: The Montale poem referenced is *"L'estate"* ("Summer").

"Book of the Dead" on page 31: The words on the outside of several rolls of papyrus containing what became called the Egyptian "Book of the Dead" can be translated "Going Forth by Day" or "Emerging Forth into the Light."

"You Want to Travel Blind" on page 33: This title is borrowed from Leonard Cohen's "Suzanne," sung by Nina Simone.

"American Flag" on page 43: The notion of "atoms belonging" alludes to Whitman's expansive gesture in "Song of Myself" where "For every atom belonging to me as good belongs to you."

"Assumption" on page 48: References Emily Dickinson's famous declaration, "If I feel physically as if the top of my head were taken off, I know *that* is poetry." The line "who looks for you" modifies the traditional "who cooks for you," as in Richard Wilbur's poem "A Barred Owl."

"Examination of Mono Lake" on page 50: The poem quoted in Part 4 is attributed to Fr. António da Ascenção Teles, parish priest of São Pedro, Portugal, site of the Capela dos Ossos.

"Politicians" on page 60: The phrase "the time is always now" is a fortuitous echo of James Baldwin's call for action in his essay "Faulkner and Desegregation," in *Nobody Knows My Name*: "There is never time in the future in which we will work out our salvation. The challenge is in the moment, the time is always now." "Politicians" was written in response to the New Hampshire Democratic Presidential Debate in 2016, which included Hilary Clinton's line, "A progressive is someone who makes progress," and, repeated by both candidates, the phrase "with all due respect."

"Lament at Exxon" on page 63: The lines "If you don't believe your body/ loves you, what can you believe?" adapts a question Robin Wall Kimmerer asks in *Braiding Sweetgrass*, where she talks of the deficit people suffer from, not knowing that the earth loves them back. The "thirty years" alludes to Exxon's knowledge since the late 1970s that burning fossil fuels causes climate change.

"Open Carry" on page 64: Alludes to Dickinson's poem "My Life had stood—a Loaded Gun. . . ." The impulse for the poem came from a comment by Mike Spies on NPR after the Las Vegas shooting: "At the core of [the NRA's] agenda is to normalize gun carrying in as many places as possible until it just becomes as natural of a thing . . . as any other accessory that people carry around."

"But Here There Are No Cows" on page 78: The title and the tone of the poem's initial question, are lifted from Robert Frost's "Mending Wall."

"Scarce from Its Mold" on page 82: The title comes from Milton's description of the Behemoth in *Paradise Lost*, VII.470.

"If This Be the Season" on page 87: The title is taken from Aristotle's *On Memory* (translated by J.I. Beare): "From milk to white, from white to mist, and thence to moist, from which one remembers Autumn (the 'season of mists'), if this be the season he is trying to recollect."

Rebecca Starks grew up in Louisville, Kentucky, earned a BA in English from Yale University and a PhD in English from Stanford University, and works as a freelance editor and as a teacher for the Osher Institute of Lifelong Learning program at the University of Vermont. Her poems and short fiction have appeared in *Baltimore Review, Ocean State Review, Slice Literary, Crab Orchard Review, Tahoma Literary Review*, and elsewhere. Winner of *Rattle*'s 2018 Neil Postman Award for Metaphor and past winner of *Poetry Northwest*'s Richard Hugo Prize, she is the founding editor-in-chief of *Mud Season Review* and a former director of the Burlington Writers Workshop. She and her family live in a log cabin in the woods of Richmond, Vermont.

ALSO FROM ABLE MUSE PRESS

Jacob M. Appel, *The Cynic in Extremis – Poems*

William Baer, *Times Square and Other Stories;*
    New Jersey Noir – A Novel;
    New Jersey Noir: Cape May – A Novel

Lee Harlin Bahan, *A Year of Mourning (Petrarch) – Translation*

Melissa Balmain, *Walking in on People (Able Muse Book Award for Poetry)*

Ben Berman, *Strange Borderlands – Poems;*
    Figuring in the Figure – Poems

Lorna Knowles Blake, *Green Hill (Able Muse Book Award for Poetry)*

Michael Cantor, *Life in the Second Circle – Poems*

Catherine Chandler, *Lines of Flight – Poems*

William Conelly, *Uncontested Grounds – Poems*

Maryann Corbett, *Credo for the Checkout Line in Winter – Poems;*
    Street View – Poems

John Philip Drury, *Sea Level Rising – Poems*

Rhina P. Espaillat, *And After All – Poems*

Anna M. Evans, *Under Dark Waters: Surviving the* Titanic *– Poems*

D. R. Goodman, *Greed: A Confession – Poems*

Margaret Ann Griffiths, *Grasshopper – The Poetry of M A Griffiths*

Katie Hartsock, *Bed of Impatiens – Poems*

Elise Hempel, *Second Rain – Poems*

Jan D. Hodge, *Taking Shape – carmina figurata;*
    The Bard & Scheherazade Keep Company – Poems

Ellen Kaufman, *House Music – Poems*

Emily Leithauser, *The Borrowed World (Able Muse Book Award for Poetry)*

Hailey Leithauser, *Saint Worm – Poems*

Carol Light, *Heaven from Steam – Poems*

Kate Light, *Character Shoes – Poems*

April Lindner, *This Bed Our Bodies Shaped – Poems*

Martin McGovern, *Bad Fame – Poems*

Jeredith Merrin, *Cup – Poems*

Richard Moore, *Selected Poems;*
    The Rule That Liberates: An Expanded Edition – Selected Essays

Richard Newman, *All the Wasted Beauty of the World – Poems*

Alfred Nicol, *Animal Psalms – Poems*

Deirdre O'Connor, *The Cupped Field (Able Muse Book Award for Poetry)*

Frank Osen, *Virtue, Big as Sin (Able Muse Book Award for Poetry)*

Alexander Pepple (Editor), *Able Muse Anthology;*
    Able Muse – a review of poetry, prose & art (semiannual, winter 2010 on)

James Pollock, *Sailing to Babylon – Poems*

Aaron Poochigian, *The Cosmic Purr – Poems;*
    Manhattanite (Able Muse Book Award for Poetry)

Tatiana Forero Puerta, *Cleaning the Ghost Room – Poems*

Jennifer Reeser, *Indigenous – Poems*

John Ridland, *Sir Gawain and the Green Knight (Anonymous) – Translation;*
    Pearl (Anonymous) – Translation

Stephen Scaer, *Pumpkin Chucking – Poems*

Hollis Seamon, *Corporeality – Stories*

Ed Shacklee, *The Blind Loon: A Bestiary*

Carrie Shipers, *Cause for Concern (Able Muse Book Award for Poetry)*

Matthew Buckley Smith, *Dirge for an Imaginary World (Able Muse Book Award for Poetry)*

Susan de Sola, *Frozen Charlotte – Poems*

Barbara Ellen Sorensen, *Compositions of the Dead Playing Flutes – Poems*

Sally Thomas, *Motherland – Poems*

Rosemerry Wahtola Trommer, *Naked for Tea – Poems*

Wendy Videlock, *Slingshots and Love Plums – Poems;*
    The Dark Gnu and Other Poems;
    Nevertheless – Poems

Richard Wakefield, *A Vertical Mile – Poems*

Gail White, *Asperity Street – Poems*

Chelsea Woodard, *Vellum – Poems*

www.ablemusepress.com

.

www.ingramcontent.com/pod-product-compliance
Lightning Source LLC
Chambersburg PA
CBHW021406090426
42742CB00009B/1037